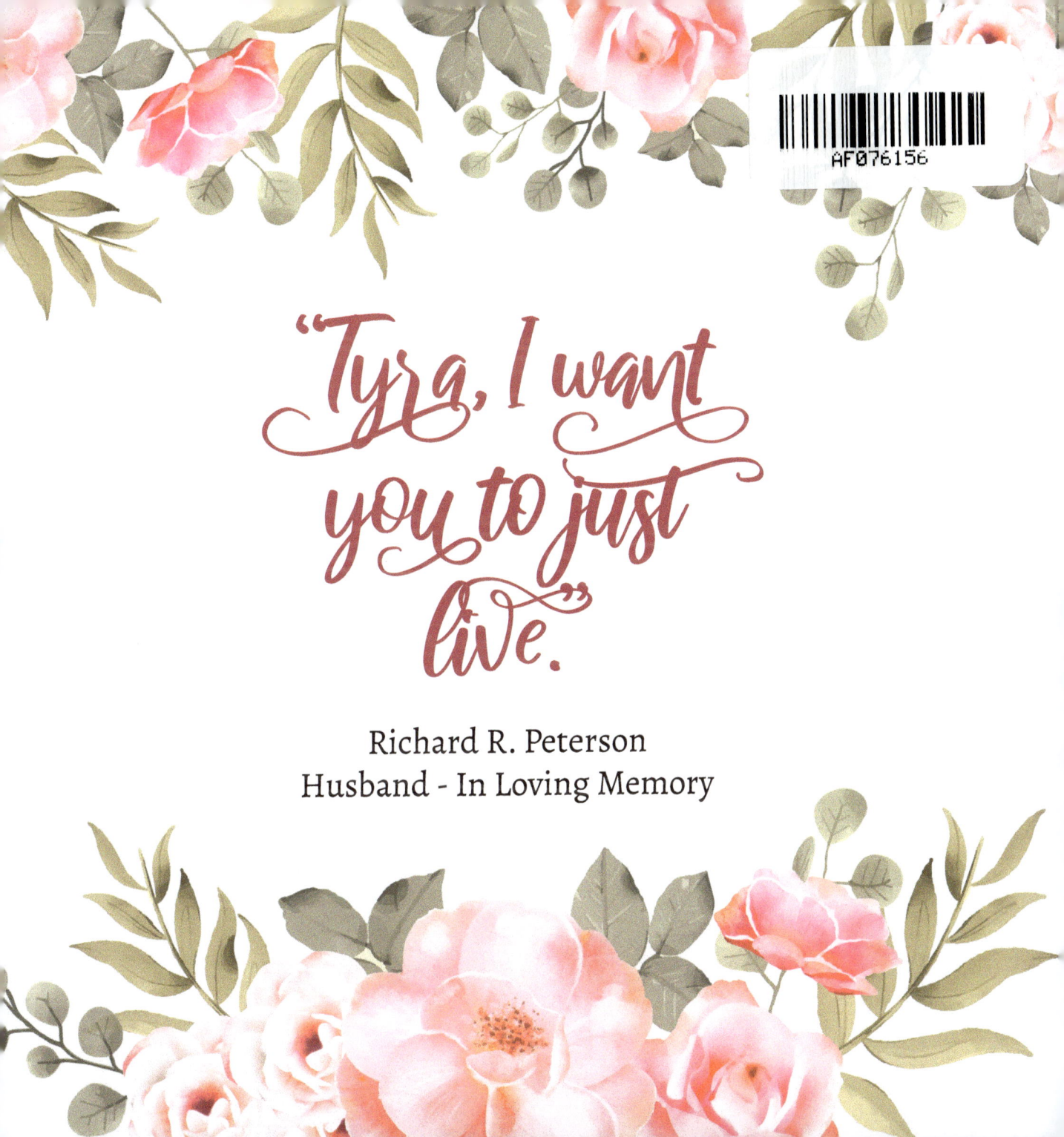

Copyright © 2020 Ché Peterson

All rights reserved. No part of this publication may be reproduced, distributed, or transmitted in any form or by any means, including photocopying, recording, or other electronic or mechanical methods, without the prior written permission of the publisher, except in the case of brief quotations embodied in critical reviews and certain oth-er noncommercial uses permitted by copyright law. For permission requests, write to the publisher at: jai@jaipublishing.com

Ordering Information: Quantity sales. Special discounts are available on quantity purchases by corporations, associations, and others. For details, contact the publisher at the electronic address above.

Scripture taken from the New King James Version®. Copyright © 1982 by Thomas Nelson. Used by permission. All rights reserved.

Layout and design by: Worrda 77 / Guru

ISBN: 978-1-7352082-6-8

Image by Dung Tran from Pixabay; Image by MR1313 from Pixabay; Image by Natali Lazebina from Pixabay; Image by Kenya Aguirre from Pixabay; Image by Werner Weisser from Pixabay; Image by Alexander Lesnitsky from Pixabay; Images by Vectorium / Freepik; Image by BiZkettE1 / Freepik; Image Designed by Freepik

Manifestation Mirror

Do-It-Yourself Guide to Full Manifestation
The Key To Getting What You Want Out of Life

CHÉ PETERSON

Dedication

I dedicate this book to all of my friends and loved ones. Thank you for your unwavering support.

And to God for giving me this beautiful idea and for visiting me each morning as I prepare myself for the day.

Contents

Letter From Ché	7
Step 1: Supplies	15
Inside My Mirror	27
Step 2: Take a Look in the Mirror	35
Step 3: Make a Room	55
Step 4: Manifest!	73
Last Step: Becoming YOU	89

Letter From Ché

This idea came to me sometime last year about making a mirror of manifestation. I had to do my research about what manifestation was and making sure that I wasn't embarking on some type of witch-craft, you know, or some type of religious ritual so I wouldn't experi-ence any of that backlash.

My heart's desire for the Manifestation Mirror is to encourage women and men to design their own mirror, so they can see themselves as they are manifesting into their own lives—the life and success that they are pursuing.

Manifestation have been mentioned in the Bible by *putting on garments* in the supernatural sense.

What does manifestation mean to me? It means to speak and to believe something into existence. Webster's dictionary describes it as:

MAN·I·FES·TA·TION

/ˌmanəfəˈstāSH(ə)n, ˌmanəˌfesˈtāSH(ə)n / noun

an event, action, or object that clearly shows or embodies something, especially a theory or an abstract idea.

Here's what I'm going to do... I'm going to manifest the first thing in your life today as you're reading: I speak into your life that you will be successful and finding the supplies needed for this project. I also speak in existence into your life the evidence of your manifestations. I believe with you that all that you ask will come to fruition. That your mind will be changed, and you will be healed of your hurt.

With that being said, let's get started!

Your Manifestation Mirror Sister,
Ché

With anything in life, the only way you know if a thing "worked" is if you test it, right? That's now. We are going to document every step we do and pay attention to the changes that we create within our lives.

So before we even get started, we want to see a "Before" and "After" picture. Before the change, and after the change.

Because if you do this right, you will notice a change yourself (and so will others)!

Post a current picture of yourself.

Don't take like a million selfies before deciding the best selfie shot go here.

Only you will see this! Keep this workbook/journal in a safe, private place where only you can access it.

BESIDES, THIS IS A PERSONAL JOURNEY.

The "Me" Before

Step 1: Supplies

List of Materials Needed

1. Picture frame of any size
2. Arts and crafts of your choice
3. E3000
4. Spray paint (optional)
5. Scissors
6. Truth and imagination
7.
8.
9.

**Feel free to improvise and add your own list of supplies here.

In order to fully dive in and be committed to creating your master-piece, you will need some supplies. You will need a picture frame of any size. I found an old frame in my garage that I used. It was 11x13 and it worked perfectly for me.

Next, you will need any arts and crafts that you want to add for your background.

I actually love glitter and bling, so of course that is what I use.

I have some pictures of my manifestation mirror at the end of this workbook.

You will also need E3000 — a very strong polymer glue that instantly holds many objects. This is best used on paper and cloth. I used a picture frame, cardboard from the post office, and the e3000 with the art supplies. I also used stencils to spray paint what I wanted on to the board. The possibilities are endless.

Remember this is your first time actually looking at yourself maybe, so you can always upgrade your manifestation mirror. Don't stress the small stuff. Do what you can. You may find trinkets along the way that you want to add to your existing mirror or you may totally redo your mirror.

You're the boss. It's your mirror.
I actually wanted someone to design for me a wooden background that says Manifestation Mirror. I'm telling you, the more I do it, the more I put into it.

You will need scissors, you will need your truth and imagination, be honest with yourself, what do you want to see? What do you want to see come to pass in your life? Accepting your healing is important.

GIVE YOURSELF PERMISSION TO HEAL!

End-of-Chapter Manifest Ex-ercise

Take about 10-20 minutes to brainstorm your Manifestation Mirror project. How will it look, what materials will you need... start making notes here.

Personal Journal

What epiphanies have you had during this exercise? Write them and meditate on them here.
Also did you see yourself improving? Growing? Or transitioning into the person you are speaking to in the mirror?

Inside My Mirror

Why did I make a mirror of manifestation for myself? Let me give you a little bit of a backstory of recent events in my life.

November 30, 2018, I lost my husband/soulmate to a motorcycle accident. After that happened, I fell into a deep depression and hon-estly I felt kind of hopeless. Before my husband's passing, this mirror of manifestation was heavy on my mind and heart, but I didn't act on it because I was too busy.

So after his passing, I began to get more and more of a nudge, or an urge, to create this book as a step-by-step guide. Little did I know, I would have to use my own mirror to heal myself after tragically los-ing my soulmate.

One morning after everything had settled, after the funeral, after all of the people who said they were going to be there for me stopped coming, I found myself looking in the mirror. I was washing my face in preparation to leave the house to handle some business for my late husband. he reflection I saw was a stranger.

My daughter had told me constantly,

"Mom you look really, really skinny. Are you okay?

Mom, please please eat something."

What I noticed in the mirror was that my daughter was actually right. I had lost so much weight, but of course I would—I wasn't eating. I was still mourning my husband. And I was convinced that it was okay for me to look like that.

But the longer I looked at myself in that bathroom mirror, the less I could recognize the image in the mirror.

I had a moment with myself in the mirror that morning.

I began to think,

"What are you doing? Why are you not eating? Do you even want to live? You can't possibly do this by yourself. You are weak. He (my late husband) was the strongest of you all."

But something happened as I looked in the mirror.

I heard a voice say,

" **You can do it, you are strong, look at you, you're beautiful.** "

Well at that time, I felt hopeless and of course I did not feel beautiful, but that voice in the back of my mind kept repeating itself as I looked at the stranger in the mirror. I wish I could say that day that I actually began to change. It didn't happen overnight. But it is happening dai-ly.

It's a progressive journey that keeps me focused on what matters. Me. You. Us. Humanity. We are in this thing called life together.

Why do some people need that nudge? Well, I would get up in the mornings, look at myself and feel worthless EVEN with all of the love that I had from my children, my husband, family and friends. So I began to speak life to myself. I would look in the mirror and tell my-self, "You're beautiful. You're going to do well today. You can con-quer anything. You're a good mother."

How many times have you've gotten up already defeated in your mind? Philippians 2:5 (King James Version) says,

"Let this mind be in you, which was also in Christ Jesus."

Now I know I am not Jesus, but if I was going to be "like" my Savior, I had to think like Him. So I began to speak to the parts of me that needed healing. I spoke life in my dead spaces.

There was a time when I was an educator in the state of Alabama that I would have my students stand in front of the mirror and sing or recite various songs to themselves.

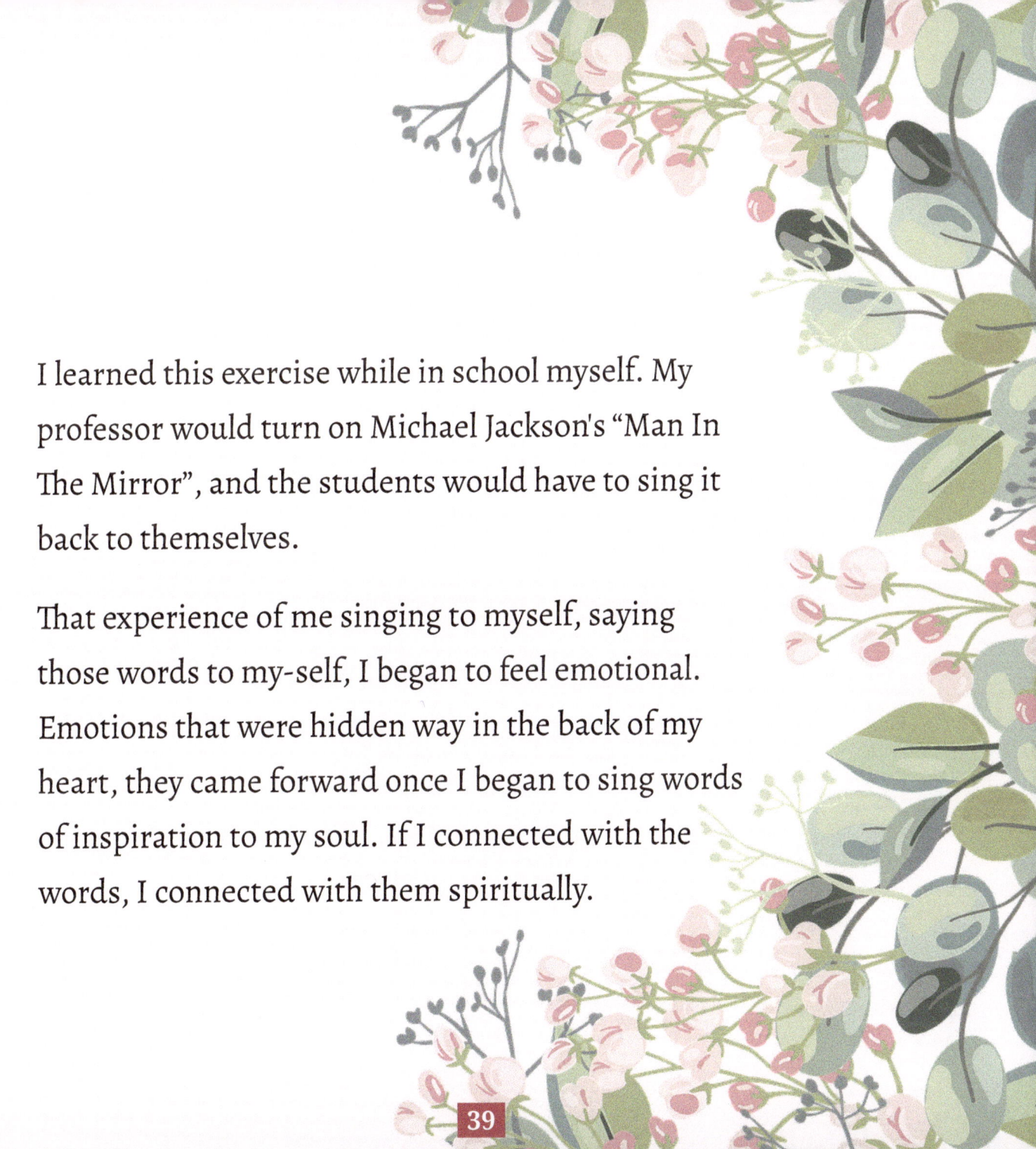

I learned this exercise while in school myself. My professor would turn on Michael Jackson's "Man In The Mirror", and the students would have to sing it back to themselves.

That experience of me singing to myself, saying those words to my-self, I began to feel emotional. Emotions that were hidden way in the back of my heart, they came forward once I began to sing words of inspiration to my soul. If I connected with the words, I connected with them spiritually.

I felt hopeful again that everything was going to be all right. Because I called forth what I wanted to see, and not what I didn't want to feel.

Now, with my students, I was teaching them the same exercise I had learned that made such a positive change in my life. What I had done differently than my teacher was that I allowed each class to vote on a song for their class to sing while standing in the mirror. Students would face themselves in the mirror, singing and crying, and

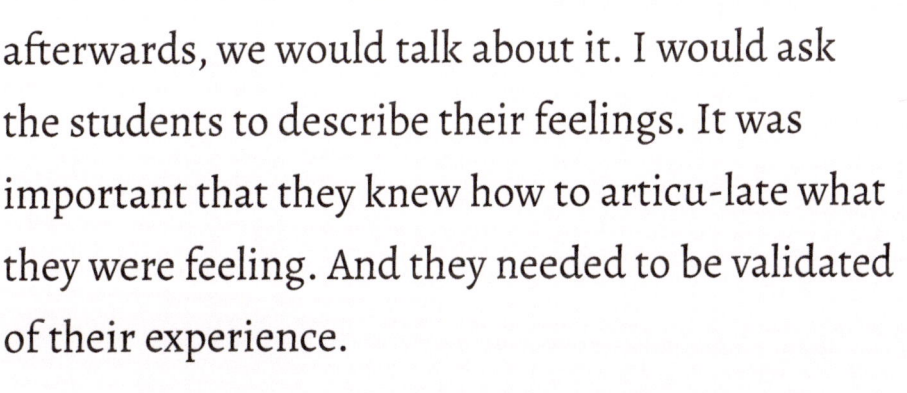

afterwards, we would talk about it. I would ask the students to describe their feelings. It was important that they knew how to articu-late what they were feeling. And they needed to be validated of their experience.

As adults, we don't often do that for our children. They want to be heard, just like us. I noticed after doing the mirror exercise with my students, they would take the initiative to come and ask me to do the mirror exercise with them!

They noticed a difference and I am sure you will, too. If you just trust the process. There's nothing like facing yourself in the mirror. There's nothing like seeing the raw you when it's just you in the mirror. How many times have you gotten up already defeated, seeing yourself in the mirror early in the morning or late in the evening (whenever you finally wake up), and hating the image looking back at you?

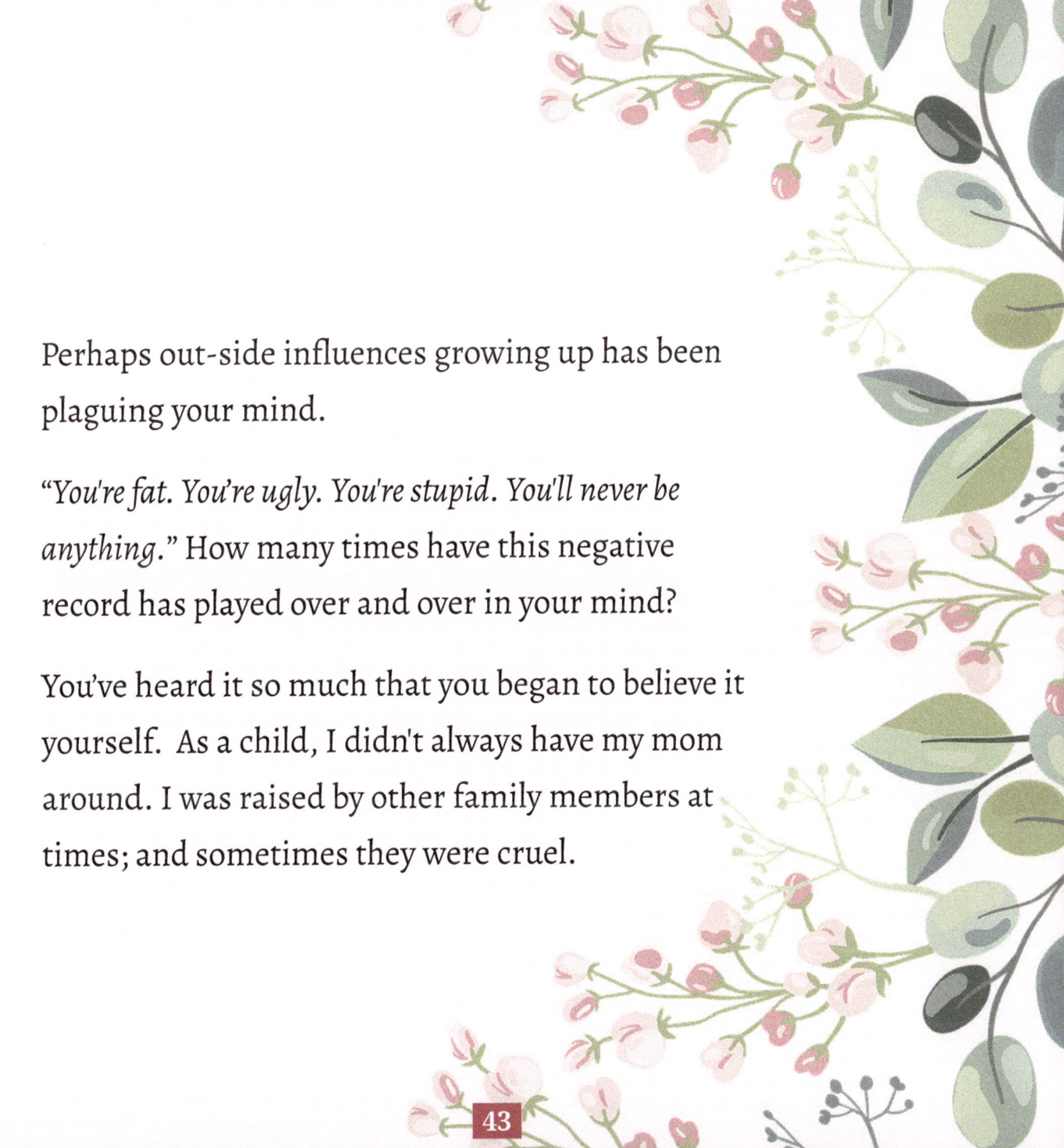

Perhaps out-side influences growing up has been plaguing your mind.

"You're fat. You're ugly. You're stupid. You'll never be anything." How many times have this negative record has played over and over in your mind?

You've heard it so much that you began to believe it yourself. As a child, I didn't always have my mom around. I was raised by other family members at times; and sometimes they were cruel.

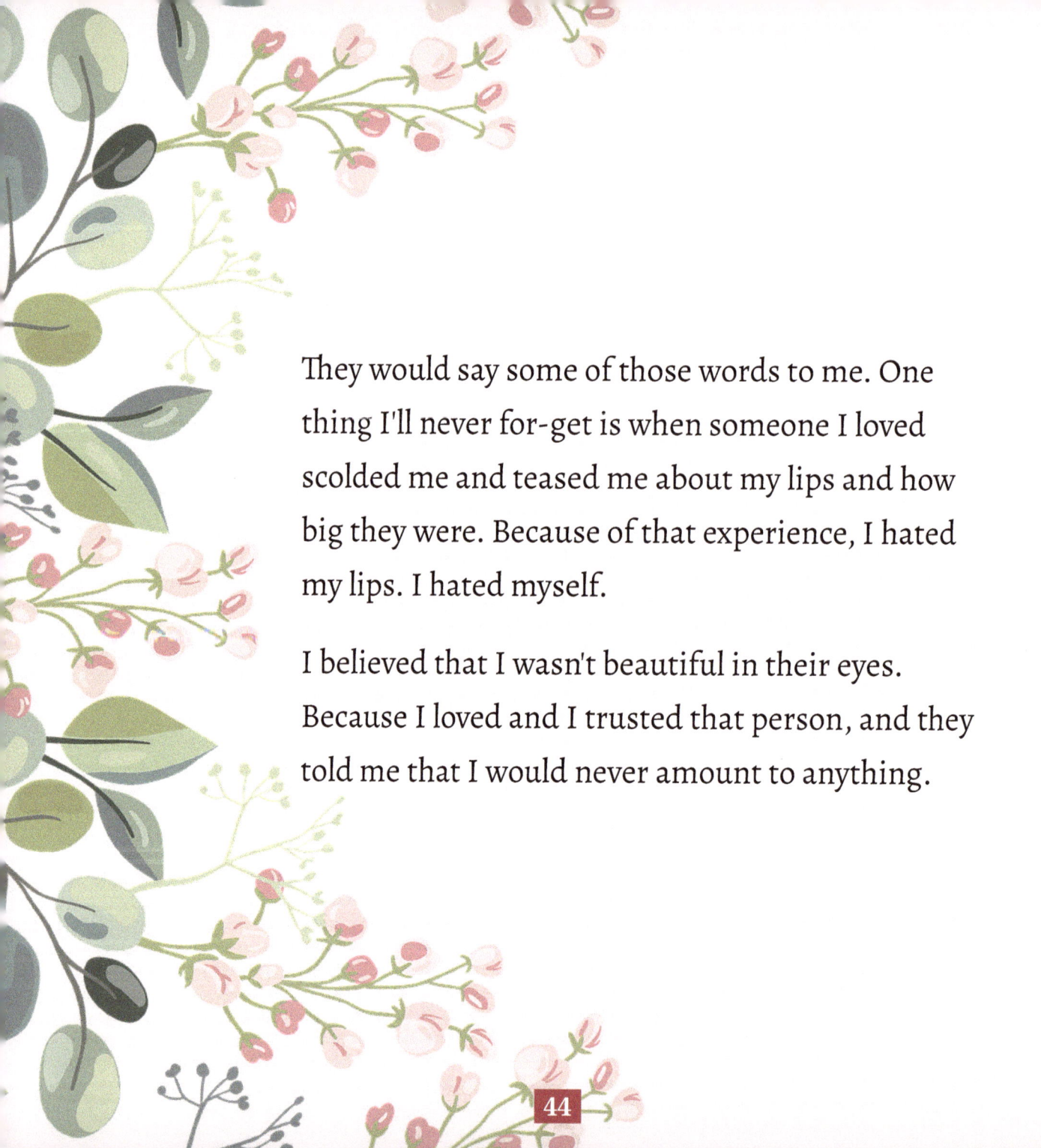

They would say some of those words to me. One thing I'll never for-get is when someone I loved scolded me and teased me about my lips and how big they were. Because of that experience, I hated my lips. I hated myself.

I believed that I wasn't beautiful in their eyes. Because I loved and I trusted that person, and they told me that I would never amount to anything.

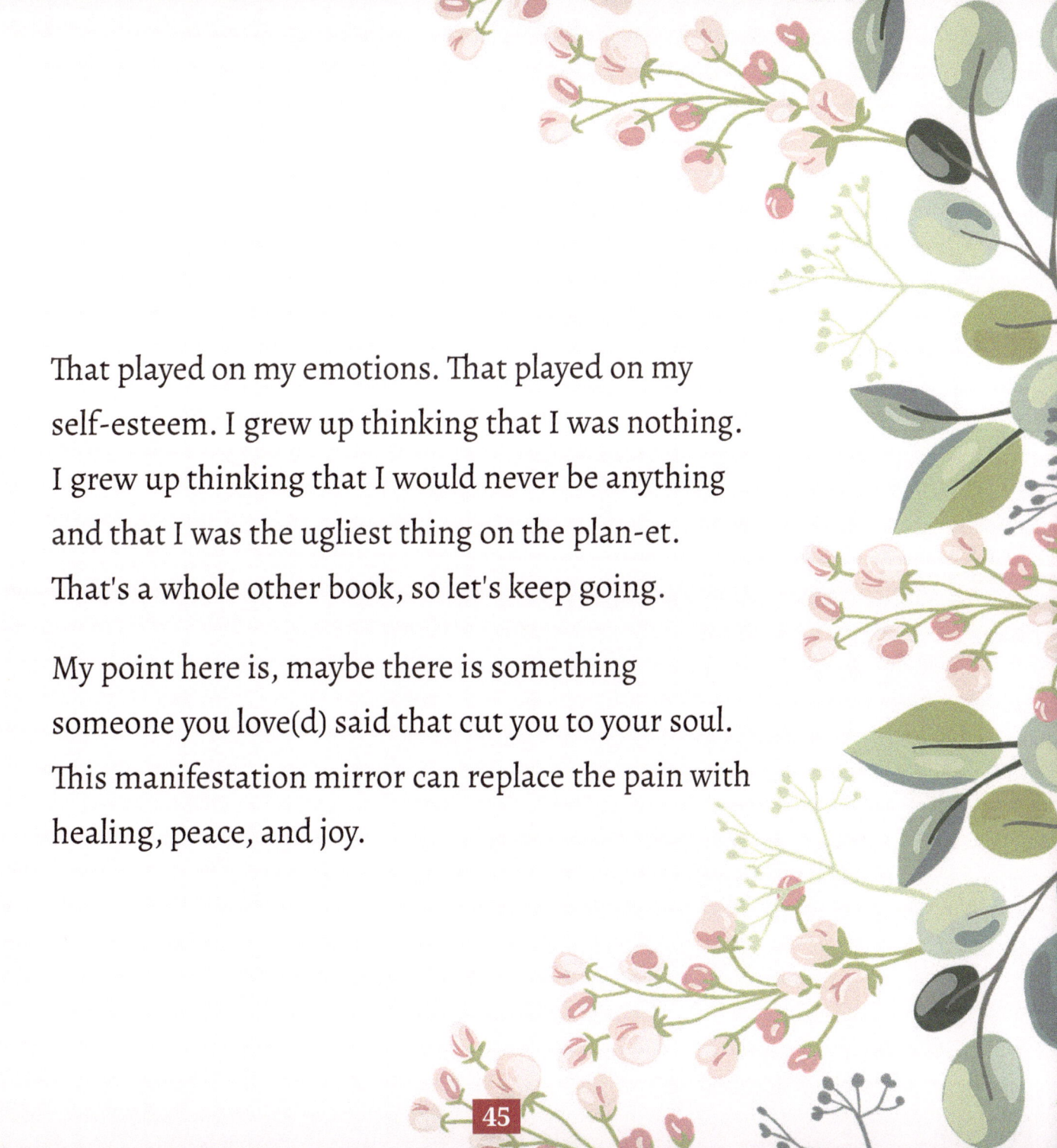

That played on my emotions. That played on my self-esteem. I grew up thinking that I was nothing. I grew up thinking that I would never be anything and that I was the ugliest thing on the plan-et. That's a whole other book, so let's keep going.

My point here is, maybe there is something someone you love(d) said that cut you to your soul. This manifestation mirror can replace the pain with healing, peace, and joy.

End-of-Chapter Manifest Ex-ercise

What were some of the words spoken to and over you that you now realize have been holding you back from living life to the fullest? Write them here. Once and for all, get them OUT of your head, OUT of your heart, on to the paper and leave it there. Free yourself from the pain of words and actions done by others or by yourself. Self-inflicted pain counts too. All emotional pain has to go. Write or post pictures in the box below..

Stumbling block(s)

Personal Journal

What epiphanies have you had during this exercise?

Write them and meditate on them here.

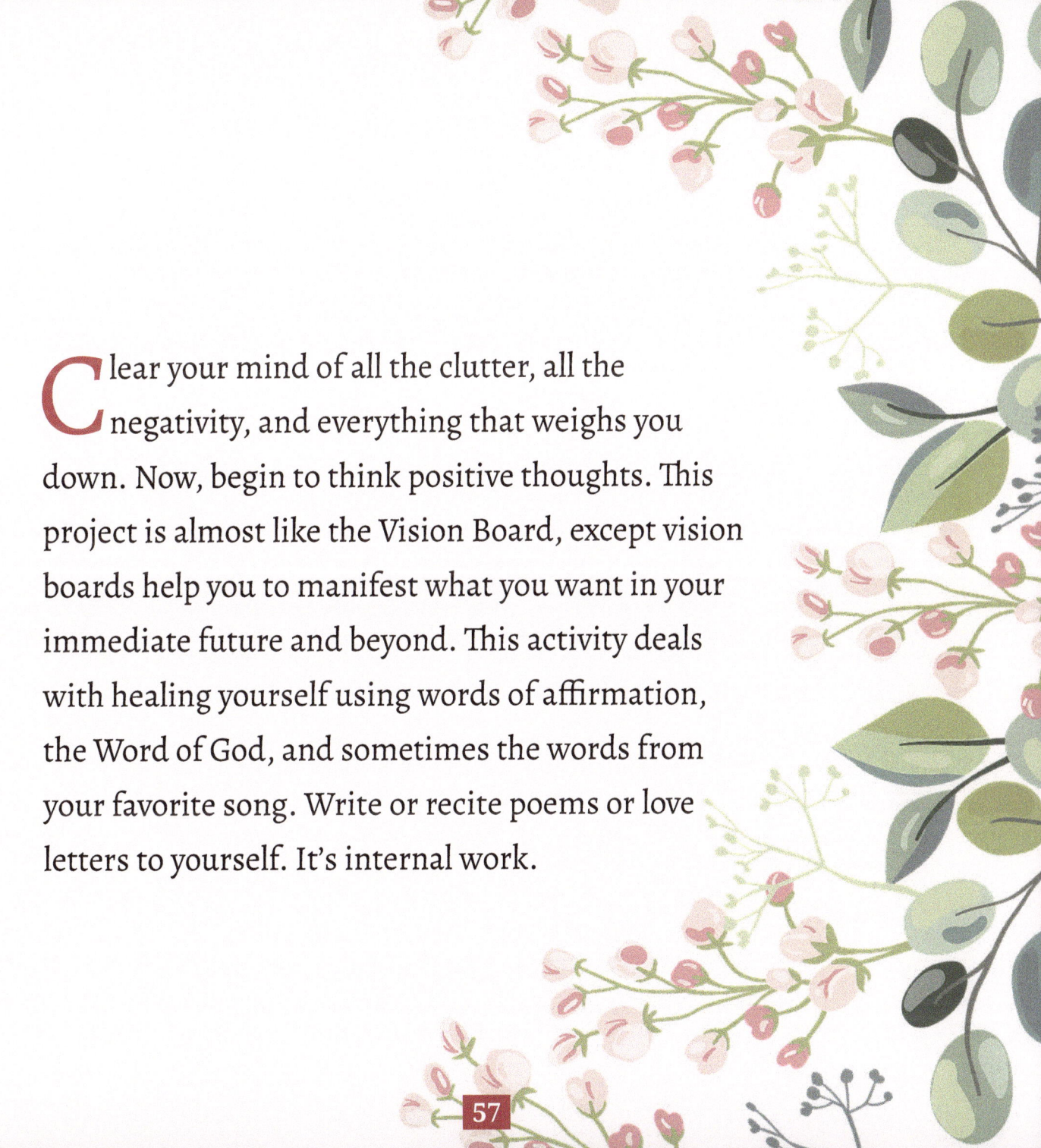

Clear your mind of all the clutter, all the negativity, and everything that weighs you down. Now, begin to think positive thoughts. This project is almost like the Vision Board, except vision boards help you to manifest what you want in your immediate future and beyond. This activity deals with healing yourself using words of affirmation, the Word of God, and sometimes the words from your favorite song. Write or recite poems or love letters to yourself. It's internal work.

You can also use arts and crafts. Rather than focus on materialistic things such as fancy cars, big houses or a pair of Balenciaga's sneakers or that pair red bottoms, you are actually rebuilding and manifesting the true love that you were born with back into your life and into your soul. What is your vision for YOU?

If anyone has ever spoken words like (or you've spoken them to yourself)

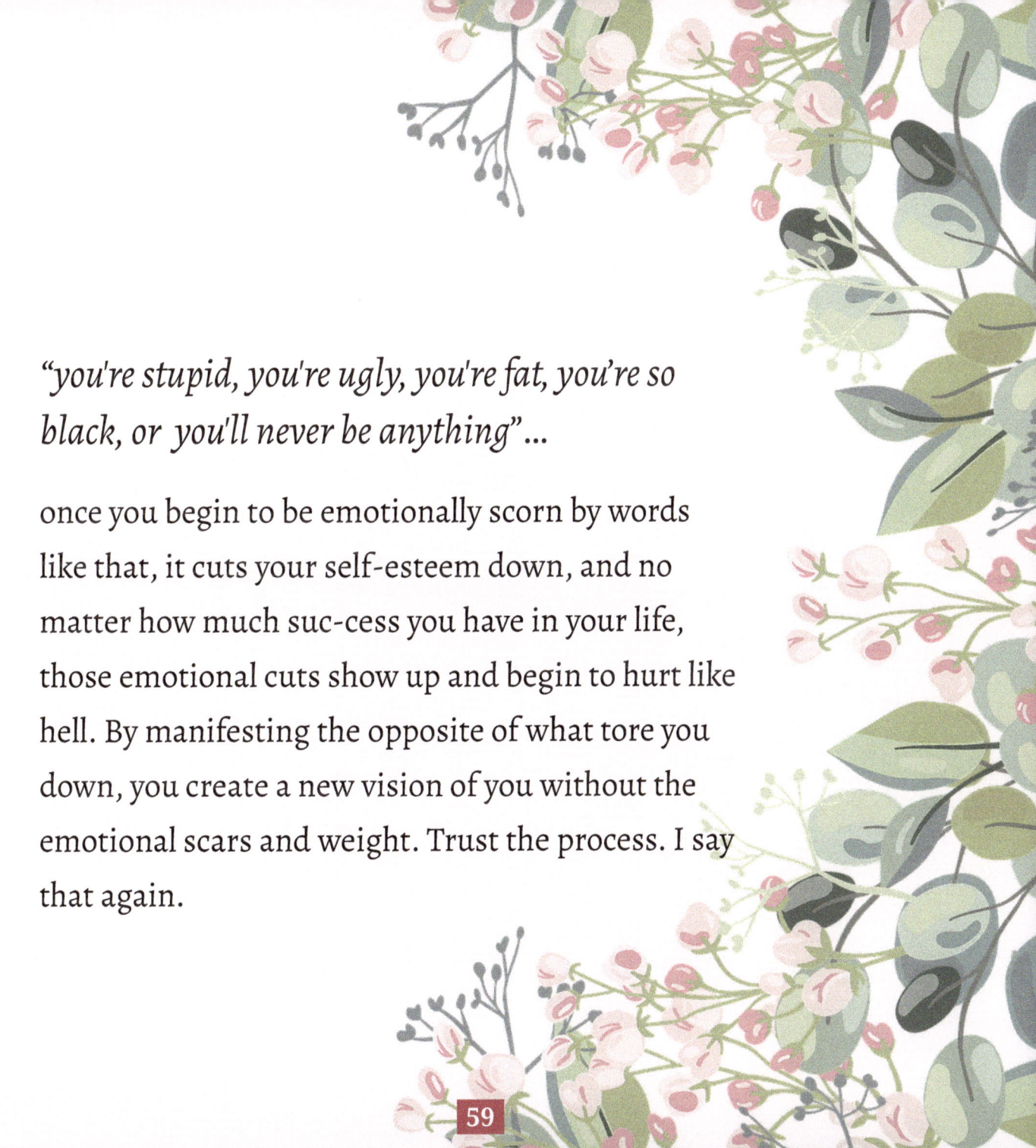

"you're stupid, you're ugly, you're fat, you're so black, or you'll never be anything"...

once you begin to be emotionally scorn by words like that, it cuts your self-esteem down, and no matter how much suc-cess you have in your life, those emotional cuts show up and begin to hurt like hell. By manifesting the opposite of what tore you down, you create a new vision of you without the emotional scars and weight. Trust the process. I say that again.

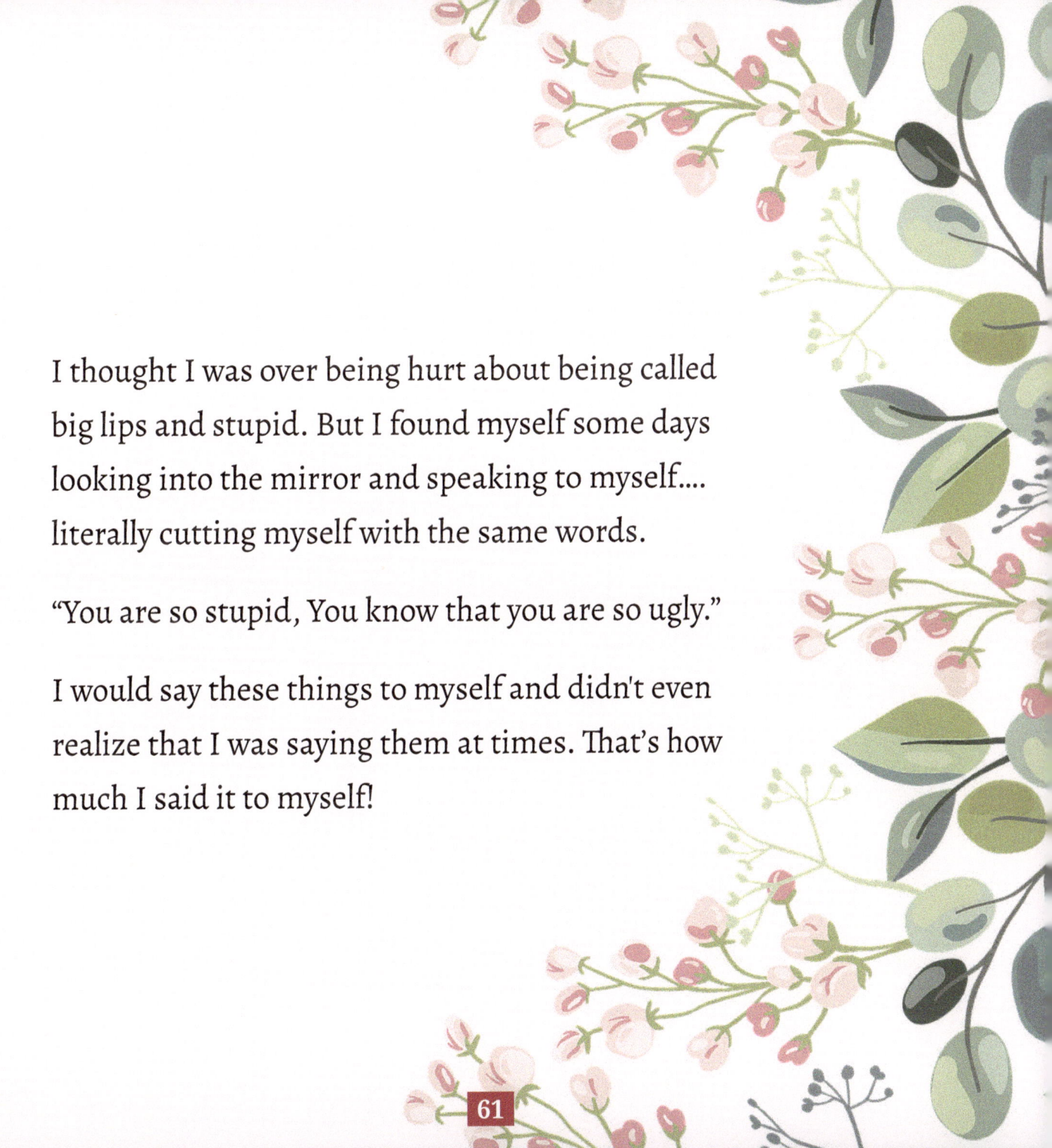

I thought I was over being hurt about being called big lips and stupid. But I found myself some days looking into the mirror and speaking to myself.... literally cutting myself with the same words.

"You are so stupid, You know that you are so ugly."

I would say these things to myself and didn't even realize that I was saying them at times. That's how much I said it to myself!

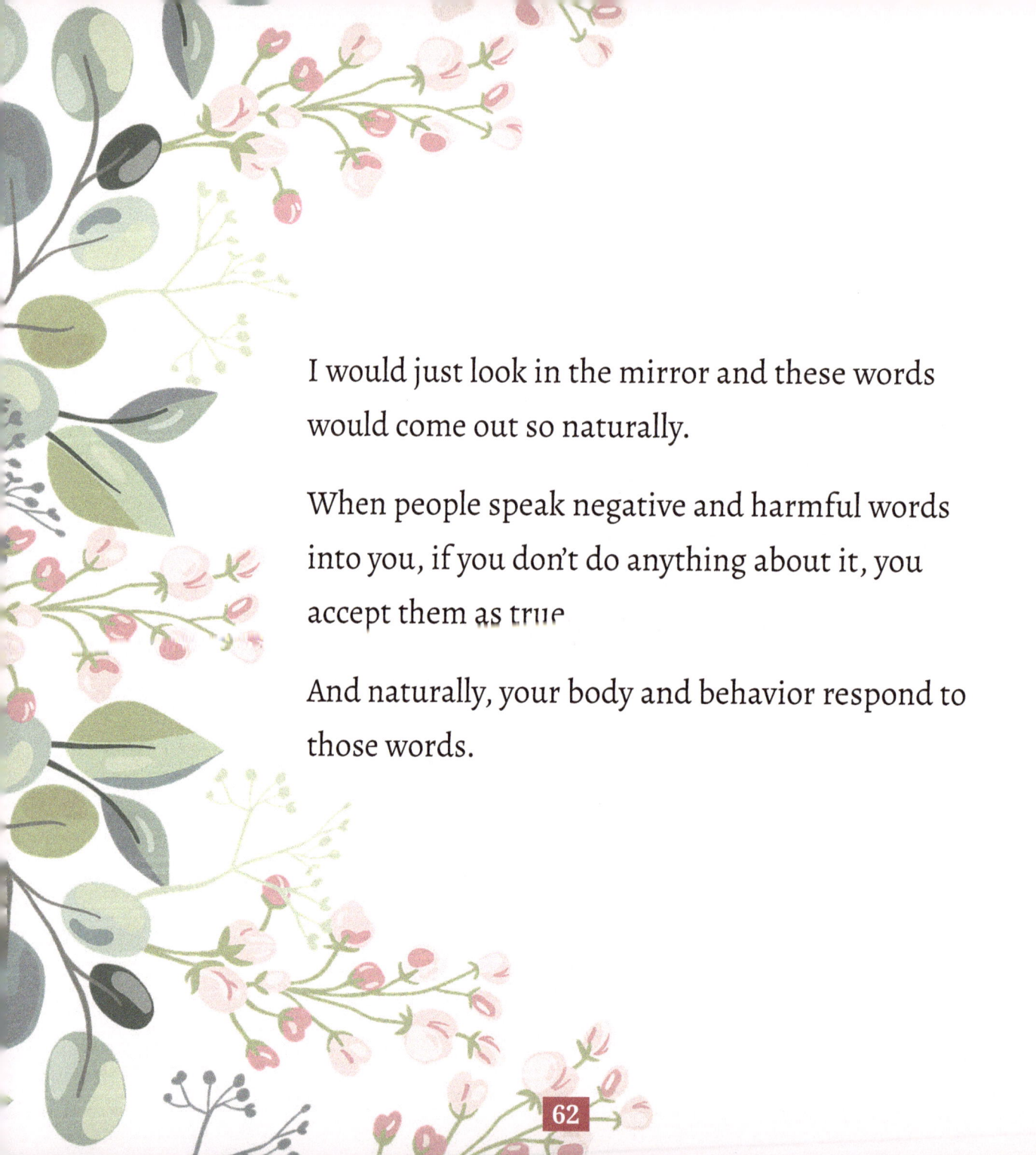

I would just look in the mirror and these words would come out so naturally.

When people speak negative and harmful words into you, if you don't do anything about it, you accept them as true.

And naturally, your body and behavior respond to those words.

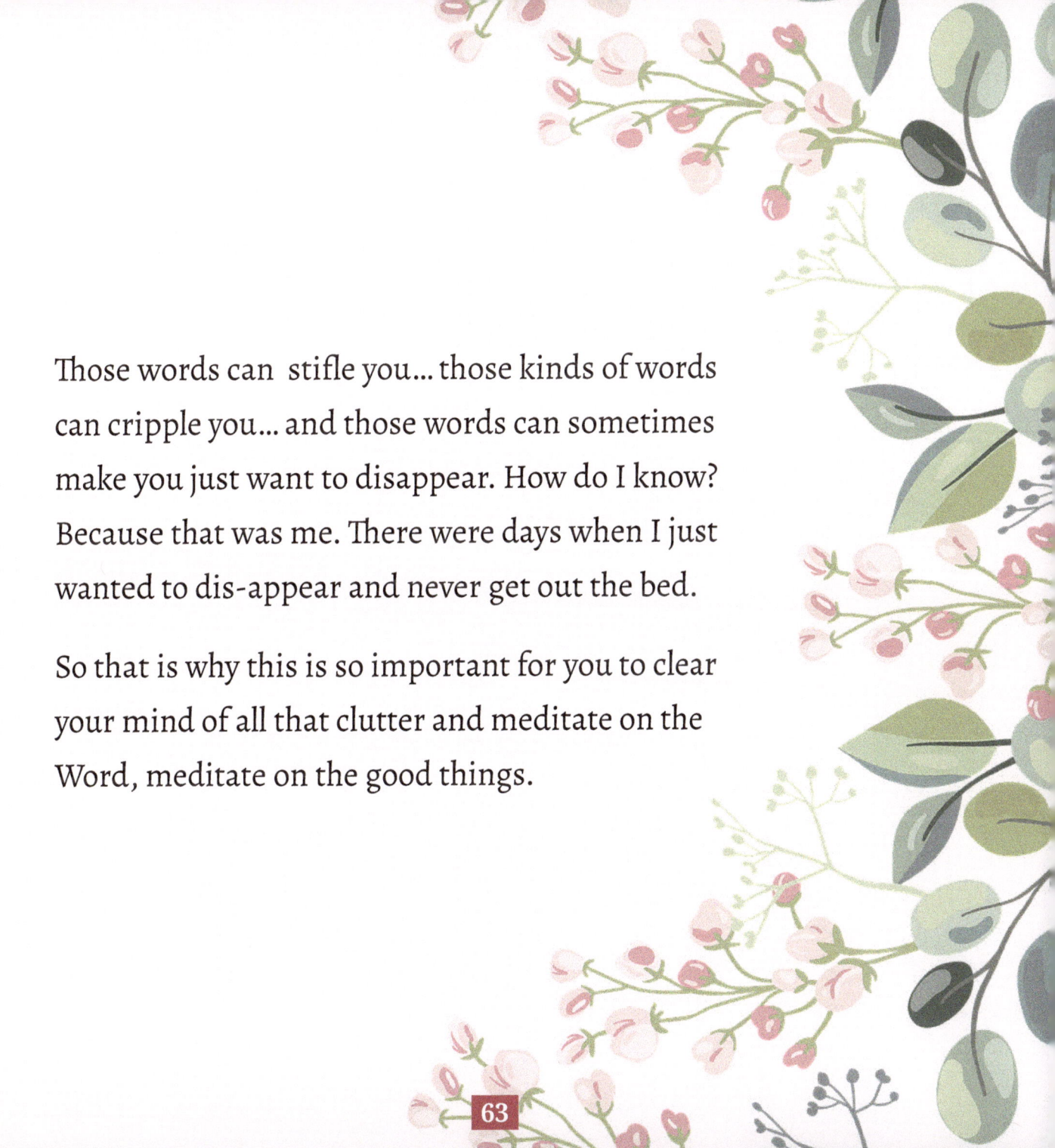

Those words can stifle you… those kinds of words can cripple you… and those words can sometimes make you just want to disappear. How do I know? Because that was me. There were days when I just wanted to dis-appear and never get out the bed.

So that is why this is so important for you to clear your mind of all that clutter and meditate on the Word, meditate on the good things.

Philippians 4:8 (KJV) says:

Finally, brethren, whatsoever things are true, whatsoever things are honest, whatsoever things are just, whatsoever things are pure, whatsoever things are lovely, whatso-ever things are of good report; if there be any virtue, and if there be any praise, think on these things.

This is what manifesting is all about. Someone had to tell you that you were beautiful. Someone had to tell you that you were smart. Someone had to tell you that you could be anything that you wanted to be. Think about those things, think on those things that are good.

And begin to write them out because these will go on to your mani-festation mirror to help you recite them back to you in order to heal the deep wounds of hurt.

End-of-Chapter Manifest Ex-ercise

Facing your truth can be challenging. Most of us hide what we really feel because it is too hurtful to accept them. But the only way to conquer your fears is to face them head on. If your feelings and emotions had a face, what would it (or they) look like?.

Now my first manifestation mirror was just the mirror in my bathroom. I would put all of the sticky notes on my bathroom mirror and die when it was time for me to clean it :). You know I had to take my sticky notes down and clean it and try to reattach some of those af-firmations that I had. Anyway, my point is, it wasn't anything fancy. Just get started, even if you don't have all of the materials I'm sug-gesting in this workbook.

Be creative within your own budget.

It's crazy because as I work on this workbook to give to you, we are in a national crisis. The world has been quarantined due to COVID-19, also known as the coronavirus. Since we have been under stay-at-home orders, I've had so much time to actually sit down and write. And even though I've found success in my business, I find myself during this time still sidetracked with just a lot of my failures.

I am applying my own precepts and methods to heal myself. That's how I know it works, because I have to resort to the manifestation mirror on days when I feel my failures are louder than my hope.

Clear your mind, sis. Clear it of all of the negative energy and nega-tive thoughts.

You'll notice that once you do that, you'll begin to think about people that have hurt you and you'll begin to forgive them. But, of course, beginning with forgiving yourself. Proverbs 23:7 says, "For as he thinketh in his heart, so is he: Eat and drink, saith he to thee; but his heart is not with thee."

Forgive yourself, see yourself healed and release yourself from the shackles of your mind and other people. When you do that, there's nothing in the world that can keep you down. What's also funny is that when I told folks that I was going to do this book, they didn't see the vision as I did.

They couldn't get pass the vision board idea with a board and a bunch of sticky notes. But the manifestation mirror concept was not for them. And if you're holding this book in your hand now, then you are who this is for. You'll get it. You'll understand it. And you'll use it to your advantage.

The manifestation mirror is not a magic mirror… it is something for you to take your mind off all the negativity and to put love into this mirror, so when you look into the mirror everyday, you'll get love back in return. You loving you. A daily reminder to love yourself. Be-cause you deserve it.

One of my favorite shows is RuPaul's Drag Race. And RuPaul al-ways says, "If you can't love yourself, how in the hell you're gonna love somebody else? Can I get an Amen?" That is one of the realest statements I've heard. This mirror is about finding your love for you, not being validated by anyone else, and healing those deep scars that are there.

End-of-Chapter Manifest Ex-ercise

Facing your truth can be challenging. Most of us hide what we really feel because it is too hurtful to accept them. But the only way to conquer your fears is to face them head on. If your feelings and emotions had a face, what would it (or they) look like?.

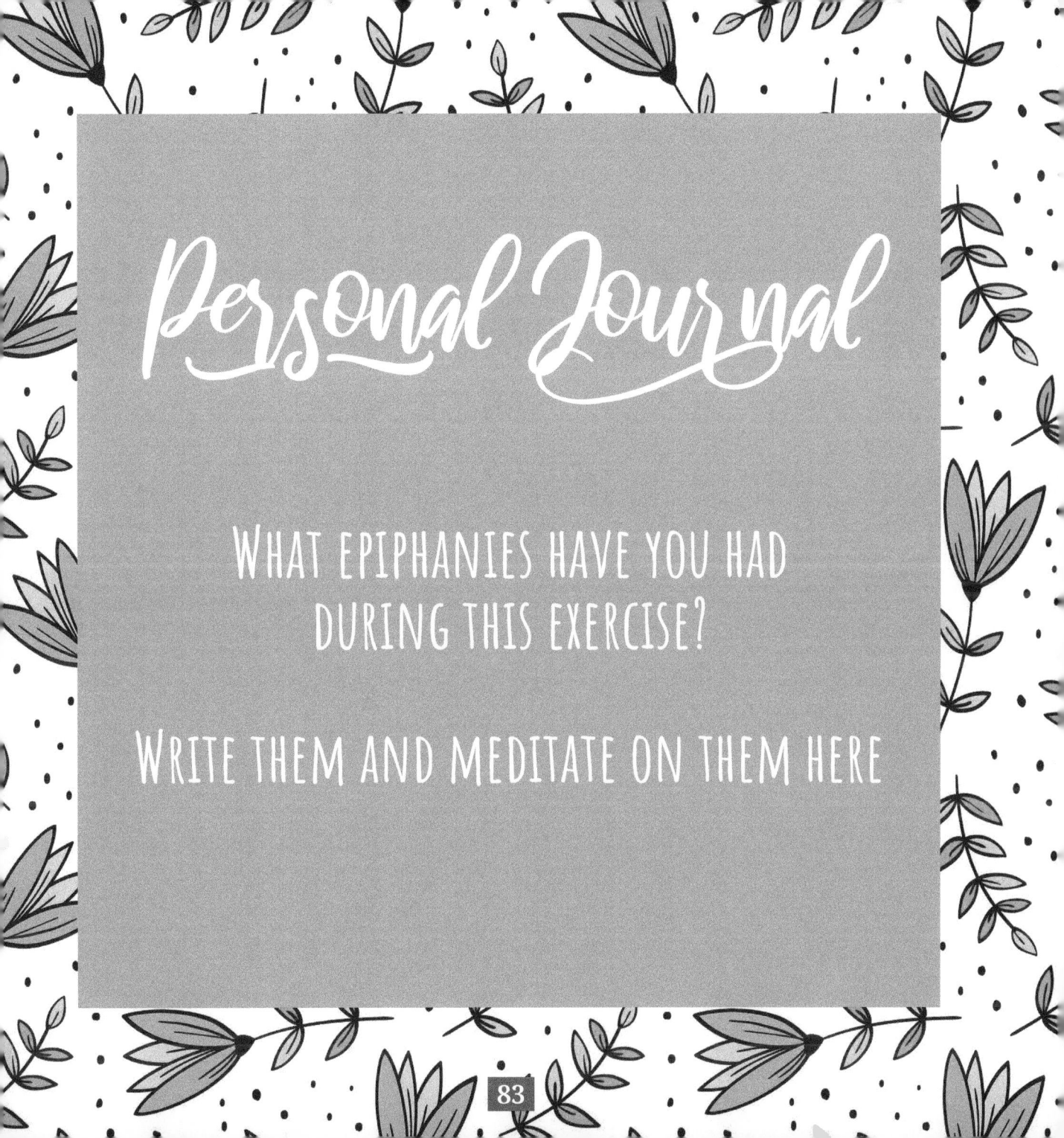

Personal Journal

What epiphanies have you had during this exercise?

Write them and meditate on them here

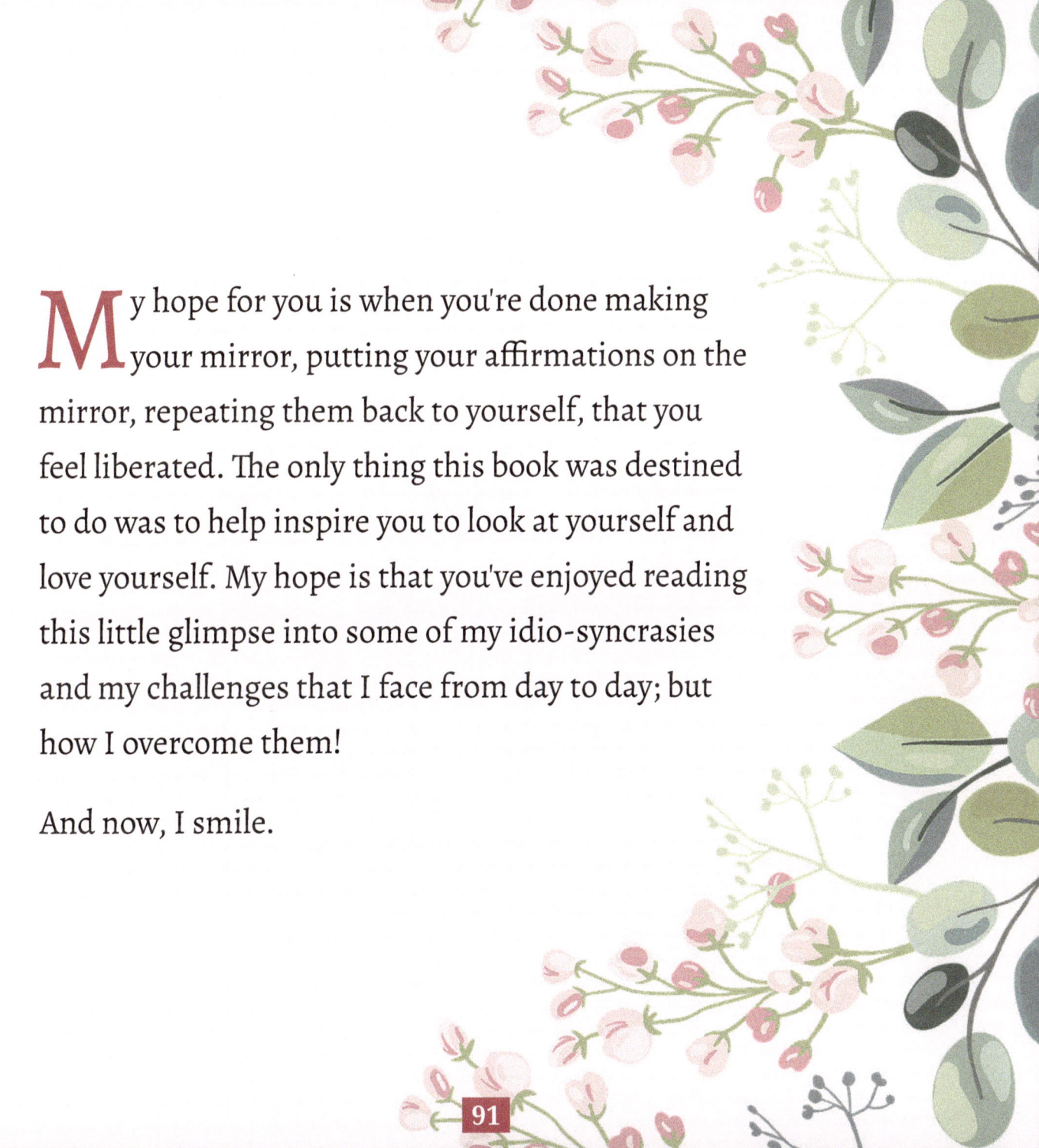

My hope for you is when you're done making your mirror, putting your affirmations on the mirror, repeating them back to yourself, that you feel liberated. The only thing this book was destined to do was to help inspire you to look at yourself and love yourself. My hope is that you've enjoyed reading this little glimpse into some of my idio-syncrasies and my challenges that I face from day to day; but how I overcome them!

And now, I smile.

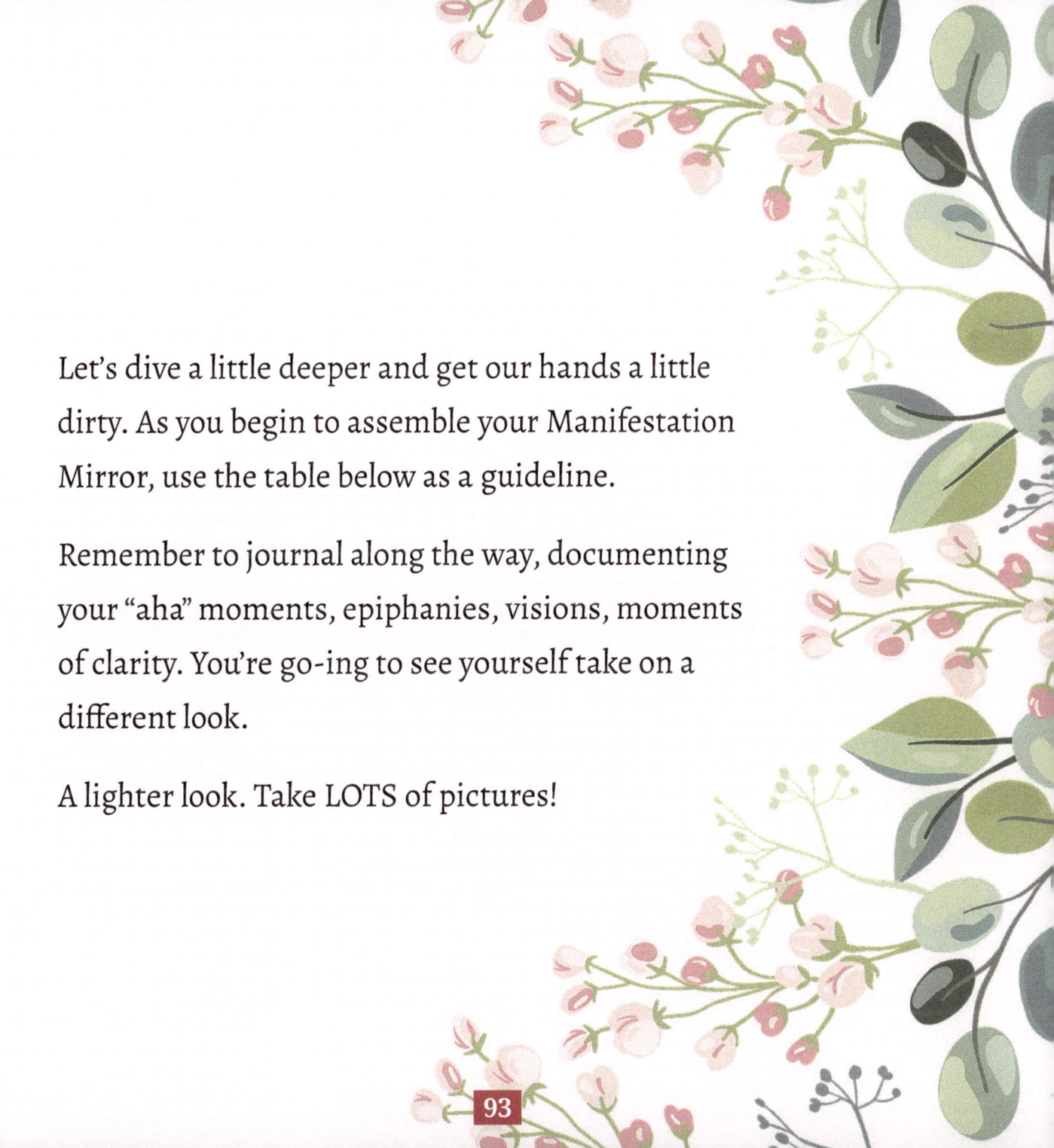

Let's dive a little deeper and get our hands a little dirty. As you begin to assemble your Manifestation Mirror, use the table below as a guideline.

Remember to journal along the way, documenting your "aha" moments, epiphanies, visions, moments of clarity. You're go-ing to see yourself take on a different look.

A lighter look. Take LOTS of pictures!

Assembling Your Manifestation Mirror Exercise

SELF-CARE BINGO CHART

Do Yoga in the Sunhine	Unplug from Technology	Read a Book	Take a Bubble Bath	Make a Summer Playlist
Go out for ice cream	Go for a long walk or run	Visit your favorite store	Have a picnic	Go for a swim
Binge-watch your favorite series	Sit in your backyard and stargaze	Put *yourself* First	Take a daytime nap	Meditate
Say NO	Make homemade ice cream	Take a long drive alone	Stretch your body	Repeat daily affirmations
Say YES to something new	Go for a pedicure	Bay yourself a cupcake	Go out to dinner alone	Call your best friend to talk

CHÉ MANIFESTATION MIRROR PROJECT

The "Me" After

About the Author

Style. Beauty. Exquisite. A mother of 3 beautiful children and 3 rambunctious dogs. Raised from the concrete jungles of Philadelphia, Pennsylvania to a California Girl, now settled in the heart of Pensacola. A military spouse and widow. This is just the tip of the iceberg of the story of Mrs. Che' Peterson. She's true beauty inside and out.

Che' Peterson is the Master Stylist and CEO of Platinum Hair Design Studio located in Pensacola, Florida. She spent years traveling from coast to coast, learning all there is to know about hair, while keeping up with the latest trends.

Seeing a need in the industry to represent people of color, Che' became certified in the Metowi Method Weave installation and offers InvisaBlend for clients who struggle with extremely thin hair! It is her passion to help women feel beautiful that drives her core mission at her hair salon and even in her personal life.

When you visit Che', you are sure to walk away with confidence and inspiration to be the great and amazing soul you already are!

Whether Che' is giving you a short sassy haircut or a long and classy style, it will be an experience you won't forget. P

eace and tranquility is at the heart of her servitude, and it spills over into everything she does, including hair!

Follow Che' on Social Media

www.hairazadayspa.com

https://linktr.ee/platinumikonz

Facebook: PHDstudio1

Instagram: ohsheplatinum

Yelp: Platinum Hair Design Studio